your way to the

Top

The real fast track to success

by
Imah Goer

Crombie Jardine
PUBLISHING LIMITED
13 Nonsuch Walk, Cheam, Surrey, SM2 7LG
www.crombiejardine.com

This edition was first published by
Crombie Jardine Publishing Limited in 2005

Copyright © 2005, Crombie Jardine Publishing Limited

ISBN 1-905102-17-8

Written by Stewart Ferris
Cover design by Alastair Williams

Printed and bound in the United Kingdom by
William Clowes Ltd, Beccles, Suffolk

Contents

Introduction

We've all seen the tarts in the papers who sleep with someone famous and make a good living for years afterwards presenting third rate television programmes and judging pie competitions at village fêtes. We all want a slice of that pie, too, but how far do we have to go to fast track our success?

The traditional route is to study hard, work hard, stay late at the office, and collect qualifications until there are more letters after your name than there are in it. A Bachelor of Arts degree will take three or four years of studying, costing the equivalent of ten years' earnings (the actual cost of the course, accommodation, food, beer and drugs plus the amount of money you could have been earning during that time).

You then emerge with a crippling debt, a hangover like you've been hit on the head by a stalactite of frozen piss that's fallen from an aeroplane, and a vague idea of what your academic subject is all about. You have a nagging feeling that your degree is actually irrelevant to any job you might be considering, but hope that you will join a company a couple of rungs up the ladder.

The alternative is to pole vault (or whatever other sexual position you prefer) over your competitors for the job of your dreams.

Arse-licking or hard work? It's your choice...

Accountant

Description

A daring, exciting and dynamic
individual who thinks living
dangerously means submitting
tax returns at the very last minute.

Study time
4 years.

Requirements
A degree in any subject,
accounting qualifications,
and a tendency to wear beige.

The fast track alternative

FOR HIM

Make love to the examiner and make sure you ask for a receipt.

FOR HER

You may not have a good head for figures but you'll get by if your figure gives good head.

Acrobat

Description
A performer who does things
with their body that even a
rubber ball would find painful.

Study time
3 years.

Requirements
Brightly coloured tights, bare feet
and elastic bones. Plus years of
painful practice.

The fast track alternative

FOR HIM

Demonstrate bedroom acrobatics with a booking agent by shagging them upside down.

FOR HER

Perform the splits in crotchless tights in front of a booking agent.

Actor

Description
Someone who gets paid lots of
money for pretending to be
someone else for 2 hours a day.

Study time
3 years.

Requirements
Drama school, lots of
failed auditions and a part
time job as a waiter.

The fast track alternative

FOR HIM

Show the director why
you're qualified to handle
the largest part.

FOR HER

Ask if there is a 'casting couch'
and demonstrate your ability to
handle nude scenes, even
though the play doesn't have any.

Advertising executive

Description
A genius responsible for writing the advertising slogans that annoy the public so much.

Study time
1 year.

Requirements
A ponytail haircut, lots of bad ideas and a twisted view of society.

The fast track alternative

FOR HIM

Use a focus group to find out what your potential boss would like from you in bed.

FOR HER

Slip away from the focus group to give your potential employer a focus *grope*.

Airline pilot

Description

A person skilled at wearing a smart uniform, saying 'roger' and shagging stewardesses in foreign hotels.

Study time

4 years.

Requirements

A commercial aviation pilot's licence, a few hundred hours' flying time, and a little black suitcase on wheels.

The fast track alternative

FOR HIM

Get an airline boss at cruising altitude, fully pressurised and into the Mile High Club.

FOR HER

Persuade the boss that planes fly themselves anyway whilst demonstrating your skill at operating a joystick with no hands.

Architect

Description
A designer of inspiring
structures like multi-storey
car parks, drive-through
restaurants and public loos.

Study time
5 years.

Requirements
A degree, a love of concrete and
a contempt for your fellow man
and his environment.

The fast track alternative

FOR HIM

Use your pencil to redesign the examiner's interior space so that it flows organically.

FOR HER

Pretend to have dropped your pencil under the examiner's desk and redesign his trousers while you're down there.

Army captain

Description

A mid-ranking officer with responsibility for training working-class teenage recruits to die needlessly for their country.

Study time

2 years.

Requirements

A public school education, poor exam results, and a confident voice that suggests you're more intelligent than you really are.

The fast track alternative

FOR HIM

Get your privates out on parade and pump the General with your ammunition.

FOR HER

Demonstrate your capacity for polishing, loading and firing the General's rifle.

Artist

Description
A person skilled at avoiding having to work for a living – by staring at a naked model and occasionally sploshing paint onto a canvas.

Study time
3 years.

Requirements
Low academic achievements at school followed by entry into art college because nowhere else will take you.

The fast track alternative

FOR HIM

Erect a substantial easel and stroke your furry brush over a supple canvas. Or shag a client.

FOR HER

Who needs painting skills when your whole body is a work of art? Strip off in the name of culture.

Astronaut

Description
Someone who gets to ride a
thrusting rocket but then needs
help with re-entry.

Study time
12 years.

Requirements
A doctorate in astro-physics,
a jet fighter pilot's licence and
a burning desire to learn how
it feels to masturbate in
zero gravity.

The fast track alternative

FOR HIM

Demonstrate to the women of NASA that you're inherently qualified as a 'rocket man'.

FOR HER

Prove to the selection officer that even though you can't fly you can at least drive: do this by showing him how you operate a car gear stick with your mouth.

Bank manager

Description
A financial whizz-kid whose role is to refuse to lend money to people who need it, whilst offering it to those who don't.

Study time
8 years.

Requirements
Considerable banking experience and a penchant for ignoring individual circumstances and going by the rules.

The fast track alternative

FOR HIM

Show the regional manager your numeracy skills by counting her erogenous zones, plus interest.

FOR HER

Invite the regional manager to deposit his liquid assets in your private vault.

Bestselling novelist

Description

A writer who works in a cosy shed in their back garden for two hours a day and complains to their agent that they're stressed.

Study time

10 years.

Requirements

The ability to take words that are all freely available in the public domain and rearrange them into an order that people will pay for.

The fast track alternative

FOR HIM

Get a literary agent between the covers, kiss her spine and give her a happy ending.

FOR HER

Get a publisher so blind with lust for you that he doesn't notice you're illiterate: that's why there are ghost writers, after all.

Big Brother winner

Description
The last person to be voted out of the house by virtue of being (by a narrow margin) the least despicable of all the contestants.

Study time
9 weeks.

Requirements
Low intellect, poor education, uncouth manners, a dodgy haircut and a regional accent.

The fast track alternative

FOR HIM

Get caught on camera shagging the most popular bird in the house: the public will want more.

FOR HER

Slowly tease the sophisticated viewing public by revealing a little more of your body every week, culminating in a hamburger shot when you win.

Celebrity chef

Description

The twat with a bad haircut
who cooks stuff that even a
dog wouldn't want to eat.

Study time

5 years.

Requirements

A white hat, knowledge of how to
microwave a pizza and a desire
to change school dinners to
something so healthy that kids
would rather go hungry.

The fast track alternative

FOR HIM

Become a *real* naked chef by serving your meat and two veg to a hungry producer.

FOR HER

When auditioning, always taste your food like you're licking the end of the producer's dick – before swallowing.

Dentist

Description
A sadist who enjoys extracting people's molars and then expects them to make polite conversation while their mouth is full of blood and bits of metal.

Study time
4 years.

Requirements
A degree in dentistry, skill at small-talk and a big chair that goes up and down.

The fast track alternative

FOR HIM

Demonstrate that you know your way around the inside of a mouth using your tongue.

FOR HER

Climb on top of the examiner and let him anchor you in place while you polish his teeth with your nipples.

Doctor

Description
A highly respected pillar of
the community for whom
anyone will undress if asked.

Study time
7 years.

Requirements
A white coat, a confident
manner and years at
university spent cutting up
bodies and drinking Bloody
Marys made with real blood.

The fast track alternative

FOR HIM

Just put on a second hand white coat and people will queue up to undress for you.

FOR HER

Pass your medical exams by losing your stethoscope between your boobs and asking the examiner to help you find it.

English teacher

Description
Someone who knows useful stuff, like the difference between Emily and Charlotte Brontë.

Study time
3 years.

Requirements
The ability to read, drink lager and annoy local residents for three years whilst obtaining a degree in spelling.

The fast track alternative

FOR HIM

Spend four weeks learning how to give tantric massage and test it on the headmistress.

FOR HER

Squeeze the headmaster's buttocks and grin suggestively.

Entrepreneur

Description

A self-employed wheeler-dealer
who starts life as a market trader
then expands into businesses
that sell goods of legal origin.

Study time
1 year.

Requirements
An eye for a bargain, a big coat
and an understanding of the
concept that taxes do not apply
to cash earnings.

The fast track alternative

FOR HIM

Earn cash from the old ladies at the market with a display of your sausages, eggs and huge cock.

FOR HER

Remember that you can sell anything to any man for any price, so long as your cleavage spills out into his face.

Escort

Description
A person who gets paid for
going to parties with someone
and giving them a bit of a
seeing-to before coming home
to their own spouse.

Study time
5 days.

Requirements
Sensitivity to the needs of
the client, good social skills
and a bath once a week whether
you need one or not.

The fast track alternative

FOR HIM

An ad in the Co-op window saying 'Escort available' will get results (like people calling you to ask the mileage).

FOR HER

Reach the top of this profession by escorting an entire sports team all at once – it's a good teambuilding exercise for them.

Estate agent

Description
A compulsive liar who would sell a roofless pile of rubble as an 'airy, spacious dwelling with plenty of natural light'.

Study time
5 weeks.

Requirements
Greed, dishonesty, no knowledge of architecture whatsoever.

The fast track alternative

FOR HIM

Seduce a potential boss and convince her that your miniscule dick is deceptively spacious.

FOR HER

Put yourself on the market, making sure your main selling feature provides adequately comfortable accommodation for a potential boss.

Fashion designer

Description

A highly respected and widely
admired designer of freaky
clothes that no sane person
would ever wear.

Study time

3 years.

Requirements

A pair of scissors, a bin liner
and a pointy haircut.

The fast track alternative

FOR HIM

Get a clothes manufacturer in stitches with your wit, charm and oversized appendage.

FOR HER

Hide your lack of design talent by modelling your own range of invisible clothes in front of an eager male audience.

Fighter pilot

Description
A dashing and flamboyant character who flies to exotic countries, sees beautiful cities and bombs the hell out of them.

Study time
6 years.

Requirements
A stiff upper lip, a sense of patriotism and the ability to survive a selection process tougher than Mike Tyson.

The fast track alternative

FOR HIM

Get your chocks away with
the wing commander.

FOR HER

Offer your intimate hangar space
for the accommodation of the
selection officer's jet.

Film director

Description

The person who gets all the credit for a film even though it took 300 people to make it.

Study time

4 years.

Requirements

Film school, then directing adverts for washing powder before getting noticed by Hollywood for your ability to shout through a megaphone.

The fast track alternative

FOR HIM

Secretly film yourself shagging a Hollywood mogul, and impress (or blackmail) her with the results.

FOR HER

It doesn't matter if you point the camera back to front so long as you hold a meeting with a top producer in a jacuzzi wearing soluble swimwear.

Former child prodigy

Description
The weirdo who appears on chat
shows as a freak, with no social
skills, no friends, and a PhD
earned whilst still in the womb.

Study time
25 years.

Requirements
Obsessive parents, qualifications
earned so long ago that you
can't remember what they are,
and a confused sexuality.

The fast track alternative

FOR HIM

Buy a degree, backdate it 20 years, learn some big words and get a sex change.

FOR HER

If you look like a former child prodigy no one will sleep with you anyway, so don't bother.

Governor of California

Description

The one who has the opportunity to flex their political muscle in America's weirdest state.

Study time

30 years.

Requirements

A daily routine of 100 sit-ups, 100 weight-lifts, 100 push-ups and half a bottle of steroids.

The fast track alternative

FOR HIM

Show potential voters your toned bare bottom in a Sci-Fi film.

FOR HER

Wear a transparent top during your election campaign.

Graphic designer

Description

A dyslexic who turns to art and design as a way of hiding the inability to spell their own name.

Study time

2 years.

Requirements

A knowledge of computer graphics packages, a taste for minimalism, and an eye for design. Preferably two eyes.

The fast track alternative

FOR HIM

Give your potential employer 100 kisses, explaining that each kiss inspires 1% of your genius.

FOR HER

When presenting a bad piece of design to a client, compare it to the flawed natural beauty of the human form by taking your clothes off.

Inventor

Description
A person who invents the stuff
without which the world would
indubitably stop turning, such as
a mousemat with a clock in it.

Study time
15 years.

Requirements
A shed or workshop,
no funding and a complete
lack of inspiration.

The fast track alternative

FOR HIM

Seduce a Russian scientist, strip her naked and steal her secret plans for a Lada with a radio in it.

FOR HER

Seduce a British scientist by stroking his test tube, then steal his secret plans for a hat with a flashing light on it.

Journalist

Description
A person responsible for exaggerating, distorting and inventing the news so that no one really knows what's going on.

Study time
2 years.

Requirements
A pencil, a fertile imagination and no concern for your own popularity.

The fast track alternative

FOR HIM

Do an undercover investigation into a newspaper editor, ensuring you get under the covers with her.

FOR HER

Prepare a sample news story for the editor: an exclusive exposé of your breasts.

Juggler

Description
A person highly skilled at
throwing things into the air that
didn't need to be thrown
anywhere in the first place.

Study time
1 year.

Requirements
A set of knives, some flaming
torches and a higher than
average number of balls.

The fast track alternative

FOR HIM

If seduction fails, threaten to practise knife throwing on the circus owner.

FOR HER

Demonstrate to the circus owner your skill in handling balls without actually throwing anything.

King/Queen

Description
A well-paid person who pretends to run a country but actually doesn't have to do anything except live in big castles and kill foxes for fun.

Study time
500 years.

Requirements
Violent, self-serving ancestors who murdered their monarch and proclaimed themselves rulers appointed by God Himself.

The fast track alternative

FOR HIM

Become a bodyguard to a princess and guard her so intimately that she marries you.

FOR HER

Seduce a prince and don't make the mistake of leaving him every time he's unfaithful: stick it out until you're queen.

Lawyer

Description
An obese, gout-ridden port
drinker who makes a fortune
from the misfortunes of others.

Study time
5 years.

Requirements
A degree plus postgraduate law
qualifications, wealthy parents
and a pinstriped suit.

The fast track alternative

FOR HIM

Pull down your briefs for the boss and lodge an injunction that gets upheld all night long.

FOR HER

Spill a glass of port on the boss's pinstriped trousers then slowly lick it clean until his case comes up.

Lion tamer

Description

An idiot who forgot to visit the
careers advisor at school and
ends up earning a living from
sticking their head in a hungry
carnivore's mouth.

Study time

6 months.

Requirements

A small head, a small brain
and skin that doesn't taste
of cat food.

The fast track alternative

FOR HIM

Let the beast in you give the circus owner a thrilling ride.

FOR HER

Prove you can do the job by showing the ring master how you tamed your pussy.

Local radio DJ

Description
A crucial member of society,
without whose inane daily
broadcast banter civilisation
would surely crumble.

Study time
1 year.

Requirements
Knowledge of the mixing deck,
skill at talking to morons during
phone-ins and enthusiasm
for bland music.

The fast track alternative

FOR HIM

Impress the boss by talking bollocks for so long that she grabs them and offers you a slot.

FOR HER

Show the station boss that you can work his microphone, his fader, his knob – whatever you want to call it.

Lottery winner

Description
A person who experiences a
sudden windfall of cash and an
equally sudden replacement of
genuine friends with freeloaders.

Study time
1 week.

Requirements
Just buy a ticket and pick
the correct numbers.
What could be easier?

The fast track alternative

FOR HIM

Charm your way into a lottery winner's knickers and don't emerge until your tongue goes into spasm.

FOR HER

Get a job handing over winners' cheques and congratulate them with a kiss they won't forget.

Magician

Description
A fraudster who can't really do magic at all: believe it or not, everything they do is a sly trick designed to mislead an audience.

Study time
2 years.

Requirements
Sleeves big enough to accommodate a rabbit, a dove, a pack of cards, multi-coloured hankies and a glass of water.

The fast track alternative

FOR HIM

Get a venue manager to give you a gig by working magic on her with your wand.

FOR HER

Dress in a spangly bikini that reveals so much of your body that no one sees your inept attempts at sleight of hand.

Male/female impersonator

Description
A sexually obscure performer popular with television companies for some bizarre reason.

Study time
6 weeks.

Requirements
A penchant for wearing the undergarments of the opposite sex stuffed with the appropriate vegetable enhancements.

The fast track alternative

FOR HIM

Seduce a TV mogul, and hope he's not disappointed when grapefruit falls out of your bra.

FOR HER

Seduce a TV mogul, and hope she can think of something fun to do with the banana in your pants.

Mathematician

Description
A brainbox who spends years at the taxpayers' expense learning to do what a cheap plastic calculator can do in seconds.

Study time
3 years.

Requirements
A degree in mathematics, wire-rimmed glasses and a beaky nose.

The fast track alternative

FOR HIM

Calculate your chances of being able to seduce the examiner: the correct answer is zero.

FOR HER

Show the examiner how to count in base 2 using your pendulous breasts instead of an abacus.

Mayor/Mayoress

Description

That local politician with not much extra power, not much extra money, but with plenty of bling to wear as part of the uniform.

Study time

25 years.

Requirements

A lifetime wasted in local politics deciding on civic matters such as how many bins the city centre should have.

The fast track alternative

FOR HIM

Shag the local party leaders wearing nothing but bling around your neck until they get the hint.

FOR HER

Just shag the mayor, make him leave his wife, and hey presto you're the mayoress.

Model

Description
Someone who has the body
of a god or goddess combined
with the intellectual capacity
of a tomato.

Study time
5 minutes.

Requirements
The ability to exist on a diet
of water and hard drugs,
look moody and wear
expensive clothes.

The fast track alternative

FOR HIM

A 69 with the manageress of a model agency will help, provided she can count that high.

FOR HER

Stripping off for a talent scout is sure to help, and if he gets hot under the collar make sure you help him remove his woggle.

Newspaper editor

Description
A biased, opinionated, bad-tempered despot who controls the current affairs knowledge of a large chunk of the population.

Study time
20 years.

Requirements
A lifetime in the business, extreme right wing views and no real editing skills at all.

The fast track alternative

FOR HIM

Show a newspaper owner you're right for the job by shagging her within a tight deadline.

FOR HER

Use your body to show the boss your plans to roll out *Page 3* into other parts of the paper.

Newsreader

Description
A highly skilled person capable
of sitting at a desk and reading
words off a screen, sometimes
for up to half an hour per day.

Study time
7 years.

Requirements
Basic literacy, journalistic
experience and a trademark
wink or burp to end each report.

The fast track alternative

FOR HIM

Make the boss the main news of the day by covering all of her main points . . . in cream.

FOR HER

At the audition request that the producer in charge personally fits your radio mike up through your capacious bra.

Opera singer

Description
A really fat person who sings like they've got a small dog stuck in their throat.

Study time
8 years.

Requirements
Regular singing tuition, eating pies and trying to understand how people can enjoy opera without first injecting recreational pharmaceuticals into their veins.

The fast track alternative

FOR HIM

Eat 100 pies then massage the opera director's naked body with your enhanced belly.

FOR HER

Remove the small dog from your throat and replace it with the opera director's baton.

Photographer

Description

The much envied person
responsible for taking
artistic photos of subjects
of great public interest like
birds with their wabs out.

Study time
2 years.

Requirements

The ability to make disinterested
small talk while models undress
in front of you.

The fast track alternative

FOR HIM

Impress potential clients with the size of your zoom lens and your flash capabilities.

FOR HER

Get plenty of work by showing a portfolio of photos all featuring your naked body, some strawberries and a jug of cream.

Police detective

Description
A cool copper who gets to work in a brown raincoat that enables him to visit lap dancing clubs without the need for getting changed first.

Study time
5 years.

Requirements
A few years on the beat, a high conviction rate and a Columbo-style catchphrase.

The fast track alternative

FOR HIM

Show the chief constable that you're not afraid to take down your particulars.

FOR HER

Show the chief constable your initiatives: a raincoat with nothing underneath; and a novel place to hide a truncheon.

Pop star

Description

A singer who's at the stage in
their career when they still have
more money than sense.

Study time
5 years.

Requirements

Getting a band together, touring,
fighting, quitting the band and
going solo, getting a recording
contract, and paying for singing
lessons. In that order.

The fast track alternative

FOR HIM

Audition for Pop Idol and announce that you're gay.

FOR HER

Seduce Simon Cowell by complimenting him on his choice of trousers.

Presenter of a TV chat show

Description
A person who stops minor celebrities from plugging their ghost-written autobiographies too blatantly.

Study time
8 years.

Requirements
The ability to read autocue, introduce a band and pretend to be amused by an actor's anecdotes.

The fast track alternative

FOR HIM

Perform cunnilingus on a producer as if there is an electric eel in your mouth.

FOR HER

Inflate your breasts to twice their natural size, wear a low-cut top and bend over a lot during auditions.

President of the United States

Description
Someone whose easy job it is to
say the words 'freedom'
and 'America' over and over.

Study time
20 years.

Requirements
A father who is a former
president, a brother who controls
most of the votes and a dumb,
brainwashed electorate.

The fast track alternative

FOR HIM

Don't have sex with anyone: most of the voters think it's a sin.

FOR HER

There is no fast track: even a blow-job on a sitting (or standing) president isn't enough to make him give you his job.

Prime Minister

Description
The person with the best job in government because it comes with the comfiest swivel chair.

Study time
25 years.

Requirements
A lifetime in politics, an inability to answer questions directly, a democratic mandate and basic leadership qualities such as a full head of hair.

The fast track alternative

Impress the government Chief Whip with the size of your majority.

FOR HER

Perform fellatio on the Honourable Members.

Publisher

Description

A person highly skilled at taking
long lunches with authors
and coming up with excuses
for poor book sales.

Study time

5 years.

Requirements

A tweed jacket, a posh accent
and a permanent table reserved
at the little bistro on the corner.

The fast track alternative

FOR HIM

Display a publisher's lunching ability by nibbling a potential boss's fur pie all day long.

FOR HER

Meet a potential boss for lunch, pretend to drop your fork and don't get up from under the table until the job is yours.

Racing driver

Description
An oversexed driver who works just a handful of hours every other week and earns millions.

Study time
5 years.

Requirements
A winning record in go-cart racing or rally driving, a suit with lots of badges on it and a skill at going round corners too fast.

The fast track alternative

FOR HIM

Display your skill at negotiating tight, inside curves with a team owner's wife.

FOR HER

Show the team owner that you can save him money by providing your own twin airbags.

Rear admiral

Description
The naval officer who bravely leads the country's fighting ships into war from a warm, oak panelled office 100 miles inland.

Study time
20 years.

Requirements
100 metres swimming badge, a gruff manner and a pointy hat.

The fast track alternative

FOR HIM

Do whatever floats the boat of the chief of the Naval Academy - remember to wear a rubber ring.

FOR HER

Ask for one-to-one diving lessons and make sure that you go down head first.

Sex therapist

Description

A kind of prostitute with a
certificate on the wall and a
taxable salary.

Study time
4 years.

Requirements

Postgraduate qualifications in
oral, anal and vaginal sex
despite which you're still as bad
as everyone else in bed.

The fast track alternative

FOR HIM

Just get an office with a sign that reads 'Sex therapist – fit eye candy only' and you're in business.

FOR HER

Lie naked on a couch and let men tug their tonks over you while they whine about how their wives don't understand them. You'll make a fortune.

Spin doctor

Description
The term once referred to an
over-qualified spinner of plates
on a variety show, but now
means someone who recycles
truth into lies for the government.

Study time
3 years.

Requirements
A degree, political influence and
a belief that Pravda was a fair
and balanced newspaper.

The fast track alternative

FOR HIM

No need to shag anyone: just put a spin on your job rejection that turns it from 'no' to 'yes'.

FOR HER

Let the PM give it to you up the Khyber, then help him to deny the story to the media.

Tennis star

Description
A young person who earns
millions from playing a couple
of games of tennis a week.

Study time
12 years.

Requirements
Parents who force you
to have tennis coaching
from the age of two.

The fast track alternative

FOR HIM

Dress as a woman and play only in the ladies matches. Just like Martina Navaratilova used to do.

FOR HER

Real tennis skill is hard to fake, whoever you sleep with, but you can be a star by modelling in one those posters where the tennis totty scratches her bare arse.

Train driver

Description
A person who likes driving but just can't steer very well.

Study time
6 weeks.

Requirements
A passion for locomotives, a love of railway station graffiti and a hobby that involves spotting faecal deposits on the tracks.

The fast track alternative

FOR HIM

Couple with a railway boss in the sidings, but be safe: use the ticket barrier method.

FOR HER

Don't be an old boiler: jump the queue by showing that you know what a 'sleeper' is and that you don't mind getting nailed.

TV gardener

Description
An expert horticulturalist with green fingers, muddy boots and a habit of sneakily making over people's gardens without them knowing.

Study time
6 years.

Requirements
A knowledge of assorted skills ranging from flowerbed laying to stone laying to producer laying.

The fast track alternative

FOR HIM

Ensure you have the word 'tit' in both your name and your nature.

FOR HER

Just bend over in a t-shirt with no bra underneath and the job is yours.

Vet

Description
An animal lover who earns a living from cutting off puppies' knackers and administering lethal injections.

Study time
5 years.

Requirements
A degree that proves you're qualified to stick your arm up a cow's arse.

The fast track alternative

FOR HIM

Remove the cow from the end of
your arm before inserting it into
the oiled behind of an examiner.

FOR HER

Dress up in a bunny girl
outfit and let the examiner
stroke your fur.

Weather presenter

Description
Anyone who knows nothing whatsoever about meteorology, but whose face can cheer up viewers and distract them from the depressing weather.

Study time
5 minutes.

Requirements
A bubbly personality. That's about it, really!

The fast track alternative

FOR HIM

There is no shortcut
– shagging your way into this
job is the only option anyway.

FOR HER

Seduce a producer by taking him
to an isobar, letting him touch
your warm front and watching his
cumulonimbus rise.

Shag
yourself slim

The most enjoyable
way to lose weight

Imah Goer

ISBN 1-905102-03-8, £2.99

ISBN 1-905102-21-6, £2.99

ISBN 1-905102-20-8, £2.99

The Little Book of Chavs

Chavs

The Branded Guide to Britain's New Elite

LEE BOK

ISBN 1-905102-01-1, £2.99

All Crombie Jardine books are available from
High Street bookshops, Amazon or Bookpost
(P.O. Box 29, Douglas, Isle of Man, IM99 1BQ.
Tel: 01624 677237, Fax: 01624 670923,
Email: bookshop@enterprise.net.
Postage and packing free within the UK).

www.crombiejardine.com